At the Gathering of Roads

POEMS

Mohamed Gibril Sesay

Sierra Leonean Writers Series

At the Gathering of Roads

Copyright © 2016 by Mohamed Gibril Sesay
All rights reserved.

No part of this book may be reproduced in any form or by any electronic or mechanical means except by reviewers for the public press without written permission from the publishers.

ISBN: 978-99910-54-34-6

Cover Drawing: Francis Sesay

Sierra Leonean Writers Series

For Tha Iye

At the Gathering of Roads / Mohamed Gibril Sesay

Table of Contents

At the Gathering of Roads............................	1
The Big Bang of Destiny...............................	2
Little Renegades (To Burrhan)	3
Where Will Our Child Lie?.............................	5
The Man Fountain at Congo Cross..................	6
At the Gathering of Roads, ...	7
Con-Supporters..	8
I See Her	9
The Sky's A Bed	10
Strange Scenes	11
Nights Without Hearts	12
In the Stumbling Fields	14
As our Ramadan advances	16
Mama (for Tha Iye)	17
Cross of Your Love	19
At the Outdooring	21
Or Falang...	22
As our Ramadan advances	24
Money Laundered Individuals	25
We hang our heads	27
It seems to Me	30
Let's Eke It Out, Softly	33
A Festival of Press Releases	35
Sand and Sound	36
At the Gathering of Roads............................	40
Rainbow-ing of the clouds (Elections 2012)	41

At the Gathering of Roads / Mohamed Gibril Sesay

Crutches of Hope	44
I Believe	47
He Would Not Be Blackmailed	48
Let Me Be	49
I Have Seen It Before	51
As our Ramadan advances,	52
On Being Commissioned to Pray (February 1993)..	53
Aberdeen Beach	54
Waters Loll	56
We March-on	58
Wines of Memories	60
As our Ramadan advances,	61
The Raw Millennium	63
Freedom of Thought	65
Rain Dark	66
As our Ramadan advances,	67
Madam she (by Kill Them The Great)	68
September 16, 2015	70
We Tie Them Neat Neat	71
At the Gathering of Roads	72
Customs of Fell Deeds	74
Roaches Guns and Peace	76
Survival Dream	77
I shook my head; moaned	79
Orders From Below (February 1996)	80
At the Gathering of Roads	81

At the Gathering of Roads /Mohamed Gibril Sesay

POEMS ➔

At the Gathering of Roads / Mohamed Gibril Sesay

At the Gathering of Roads

At the gathering of roads
I gather myself within
Like skirts of women
Crossing a stream
This life's but a silent scream
Rumbling quick
Like holy mutterings
That divide the two halves of Juma[i] Sermon

At the Gathering of Roads / Mohamed Gibril Sesay

The Big Bang of Destiny

The Big Bang of destiny
Pushes us towards the same orbit
Of a country
We stretch our hands
To catch each other
Before our common spaces lose all gravity

We stretch hands towards each other
Before we speed forever apart
Away from earth
Away from our world
Away from from each other

The strings of memories
That bind us
Grow so thin
They become invisible
Even to ourselves
We lose sight of each other forever
Weghtless in the space of destinies
Something tugs at us
We feel it
But no longer know what it is
No longer know the person
At the other end it tugs from

At the Gathering of Roads / Mohamed Gibril Sesay

Little Renegades

Remember?
Downstairs
Near gutter
Near wall?
Papa
Was teaching us al-Qur'an
You blew ground-pepper
Towards him
He coughed
We laughed
Little renegades
Rowdy in the pain
Of your handiwork

Cleverer
Knowing Papa would cover cough
With is sacred muffler
You peppered it
He sneezed
We gamboled
He yelled
Sending
That bigmouth-without-brakes
Bumping secret into him
Knocking him crazy
He smashed walking-stick on you
THIS PIKIN[ii] GET MIND POISON ME

At the Gathering of Roads / Mohamed Gibril Sesay

We stretched you in air
As baboons a snake
But even as he flogged
He marveled at your daring
Saw his childhood in you
And remembered his father

At the Gathering of Roads /Mohamed Gibril Sesay

Where Will Our Child Lie?

Headside-footside-jamming-wall
The bed
Is workbenchwide
The room twice that
And my woman pregnant
Where will our child?

At the Gathering of Roads / Mohamed Gibril Sesay

The Man Fountain at Congo Cross

The man fountain sits
On the man-made fountain

The man fountain is gushing
The man made fountain is not

The man fountain is gushing
A life of loud complaint to passers-by

A man fountain of dishonor
A man fountain of injustice

The man fountain is out there
At Congo Cross

Still bearing the cross
Nailed on to the souls of slaves from Congo

Marooned on the shores of Freetown
The man fountain is out there

Wailing out his soul
To the soulless man made fountain

In the heart of the Peninsula
That was once called The Wailing Places

October 19, 2007

At the Gathering of Roads /Mohamed Gibril Sesay

At the Gathering of Roads,

I gather myself within,
Like skirts of girls pounding rice
Singing Inehtiba
Joyous confessions of fornication and adultery
To lighten the burden of work

At the Gathering of Roads / Mohamed Gibril Sesay

Con-Supporters

'You are a great man',
They said to him
And the small man con-taught himself
To seem great

'You can be president',
Some low-life eking for the high-life
Says to the mediocre
And the mediocre contorts himself
To look like a will-be president

I see one
With belly full of indigested beans
Full fart falling for his fart fans
His fart gatherers

I see them aplenty
Beings contorted by con-eking

At the Gathering of Roads / Mohamed Gibril Sesay

I See Her

I see her
Head held high
In the nude of her brilliance
The pubes of her new found dignity
Agonizing men of Plato's cave
Unused to such vistas of sunlight

I see them
The cave men
Writhing in masturbations
Of low sperm counts
At her cat steps

She catwalks on
Head held high
Unto her eternity of dreamed bliss

At the Gathering of Roads / Mohamed Gibril Sesay

The Sky's A Bed

The sky's a bed
My love splayed 'cross it
Full breasts glow
Like sun-dawn
Like sun-down
Gold of joy heralds beginning and end of my day
And at night, nipples sparkle stars
My fingers trace the rays to her galaxy of beauty
Her lips suck my gaze
Like some new moon sucking gazes at Ramadan's end
Welcoming me unto the soul of my rewards
Smiling out to me the new lunar month
Eid is dawned on our being

Livingstone, May 9, 2015

At the Gathering of Roads /Mohamed Gibril Sesay

Strange Scenes

Strange scenes
Of ranged sins

Tinned love
On dim-lit shelves of night
We do not see
The expiry dates
We eat in the dark

Now we retch with love poisoning

Retch sins
Of wretched scenes

At the Gathering of Roads / Mohamed Gibril Sesay

Nights Without Hearts

Our Fingers grow inward
Pushing our hearts
Away from the sick

Away from the hook of death
Tied to the line
Held by the pain of soul
Angling for compassion

Ebola

Our hearts decline
Into the Western horizon
Into the dusk of touch
Hearts lost in the night
Of the new disease

Ebola

Disorientations
In the dusk-dawn
We are tormented by the muezzin's call
Is it Subhi or Magrib?[iii]
We are confused by the imam's prostration
Is it two or three rakats?[iv]

Or is it a call
To salatu janaza?[v]

At the Gathering of Roads / Mohamed Gibril Sesay

Should we sujud[vi]
Or should we stand tall?

Ebola

The sheikhs of the new wisdom say
Monkeys are the muezzins
Of the new salatu janaza
For the unwashed corpse
The unpurified cadaver
The absentee dead

Or is it so?
Or is it bats?
What caused the Big Bang
Of this new universe of pain?

What Gibbs Particle
Make stable
The fleeting wisdoms
Of the new reality?

Stupidities about conspiracies
Conspiracies about stupidities
The dusk-dawn disorientation
Is the new moon
Of our nights without hearts

At the Gathering of Roads / Mohamed Gibril Sesay

In the Stumbling Fields

When we bring down the myths
From the nooses of the new knowledge
We find out that
They are incapable of being buried
We find out that
The myths cannot be lost
To the death of their falsehoods

The myths are now rotten-real
Too death-real to vanish:
The myth of virgins waiting in heaven to be laid
The myth of the invisible hand
The myth of trickle down economics
Of manna from the clouds
Of women finding heaven
In the cracked soles of men

Corpses of 'unbury-able' myths
Rotting in the cemeteries of our lives
We cover our noses and mouths
Muffling our words
That can not now be distinguished
From each other
We hear cuss-words within priest-words
Blast-words within blest-words
Our words have lost their boundaries
We noose our noses and mouths
In the stumbling fields

At the Gathering of Roads /Mohamed Gibril Sesay

Muffling our vigils
Our condolences too low even to be self -heard
Consolation has fled from whatsapped dirges

At the Gathering of Roads / Mohamed Gibril Sesay

As our Ramadan advances

Prayer rows at our mosques become smaller
And our scruples
Crumble into tempting viands
People-kind is created impatient
Fast-forwarding al fatiha[vii]
So as to fight over the sara[viii] of ritual murderers.

As our Ramadan advances,
Weak faith diminishes our congregations
Or, fearing the crowd we baikorkor[ix]
Don't be two bellied, the Preachers admonish,
The famished road leads to heaven's gate.

As our Ramadan advances,
My faith, my heart, falls down my stomach
Cannibalistic gastric fluids assail it.
Witches, our people say, eat their own hearts at initiation.
Am I becoming one?

At the Gathering of Roads /Mohamed Gibril Sesay

Mama
(for Tha Iye)

Mama
Wants to talk to me
But these books
Keep coming `tween us
She`ll come just as I`m
About reading a new book
Or chapter
Or paragraph
Which is about every hour
Of my house- time

I
Always want
To talk to mama
But this writing
Keeps coming `tween us
I want to talk to her
Just after this word
This phrase
O wait a little
Just this line

On evening
She says
Papa (I'm named for her father)
Why are you always reading and writing
Have you exams

At the Gathering of Roads / Mohamed Gibril Sesay

To take?

Tonight
She leans on the wicket by my door
I feel her gaze
Burrowing into my bowed scalp
It`s like her heart hollering
What book devil has taken hold of my son

She hangs on
To the tail of my eye
Wanting to get on board
My perceptions overloaded with books
Just this poem mama
I say to myself

At the Gathering of Roads / Mohamed Gibril Sesay

Cross of Your Love

Your outstretched arms
The cross of my soul

My palms nailed to your palms
Eyes glued to eyes

I'm dying on the cross
Of your body

My soul dripping
Unto the last step
I took before being nailed
Onto the vision of your love

My soul dripping
Unto the memories
Of those last free steps

Drip drip drip
Unto the freedom
Before I got myself nailed
Onto dead wood
Standing on high
Capturing the gaze
Of a lover
Wanting to fulfill a prophesy foretold

At the Gathering of Roads /Mohamed Gibril Sesay

Can I ever be brought down
From your crossed love?

Can I ever dismount
To the ascension from your pain?

At the Gathering of Roads / Mohamed Gibril Sesay

At the Outdooring

At the Outdooring of Naconquer
Gbanabom's first daughter
We eat big words
Lick our dreams
Like cats their armpits
Laughter flowing

Her head-do
Is magical
Gold glazed plaits shimmering like fish
In our flowing laughter

The granny saunters
And carelessly removes the weave-on
From the dandruff head

We glance away
Trying not to face
The muddle
In our flowing cosmeticism

Talking big about
Her French décolleté

At the Gathering of Roads / Mohamed Gibril Sesay

Or Falang[x]

Or Falang
On every journey I make
To the soul of another
Her karawas[xi] cuts my heart
And she rubs salty memories
On my heart wounds

Or falang
When I`m seeking solace
With another
She becomes her karawas

Fire on me
Fire from the stream
Fire shooting
From the stream

'To the grave'
Says the Sokobana[xii]
'The grave
To the grave
To the time of parting'

Ah there she is
As she was
Even more so
Like a shayma fu[xiii]
Smiling to me

At the Gathering of Roads / Mohamed Gibril Sesay

Healing my heart-cuts

No don`t cut[xiv]
No Sokobana
Don't cut her
Into seven places no
No
Spill not that
Un-flowing blood
Defying time
No
I want her whole

At the Gathering of Roads /Mohamed Gibril Sesay

As our Ramadan advances

Satanic roaches sulking
In the cracks of walled Ramadan thoughts

But do flies buzz an arse for naught?
Humankind is created weak, from base fluids.
And flies, even fools know, only buzz impurities.

At the Gathering of Roads / Mohamed Gibril Sesay

Money Laundered Individuals

We have seen them
The entitled ones
The money laundered individuals
Education paid for
By the loots of their fathers,
Perhaps mothers, perchance uncles, etcetera

They are beautiful
The money laundered individuals
Assets to the nation
Masters of the new destiny

We do not blame them
They are educated
With tall degrees
New assets for the damaged land

We hope these fine seeds
Grow on the craters left by the mines
We hope these good fishes
Swim in the poisoned lakes
We hope these fine buildings
Stand firm on the damaged hills

They are beautiful
With fine roses
Entitled to turn their noses
Away from the odors

At the Gathering of Roads / Mohamed Gibril Sesay

Of the people
Without the deodorants of education
Entitled to blame the people
For their lack of soap
Their lack of good English words

We cannot blame them
They are assets to the nation
Roses on the dungs of the past
They are beautiful
Clean shaven
Well versed
We look up to them
If only they do not turn away their noses

At the Gathering of Roads /Mohamed Gibril Sesay

We hang our heads

We hang our heads
On the gallows
Of her torment

Hooded by uncommon muteness
Cryptic metaphors
Secret nooses
Throttling vocal chores

In the sacred Satanism
Of resemblances
Cinna the poet
Is Cinna the conspirator

> In Arabic haram means sacred
> Means forbidden connotes satanic

Conspiracies of resemblances
Metaphors linking
Gods-to-excreta

Gandhi the holy man says
The untouchables of India
Are Harijans
- Children of God

At the Gathering of Roads / Mohamed Gibril Sesay

Gandhi's call annoyed lickers of God's toes
And they killed him
In South Africa
Gandhi called Africans
Kaffirs, unbelievers
Beneath his Harijans

Some poets too
yearn to be sacred untouchables
Like that Emperor Augustus
they think they are
celestial beings of the air
above ground, above board

Like Shakespeare's Caesar they
They loathe the soothsayer
They disdain
the sooth,

saying

mere
mire
mare

We kick away footstools

especially so
these times
So our napes are snapped
By the ropes of the expanse

At the Gathering of Roads / Mohamed Gibril Sesay

Feet dangling in the void
Of our abstractions
Our un-people-ness

At the Gathering of Roads / Mohamed Gibril Sesay

It seems to Me

It seems to me
That may, just may be, including this one,
Sweeping statements sweep too much
Why do our people say
You need not sweep at night
Is it that may be, just may be
Your night makes you sweep all -
The dirt, the clean, the not-clean enough
The not-dirty enough?

Humans rotate the orbits of their being
Humans are half day, humans are half night
As they revolve the ellipses of their destiny
Sweetest dreams happen in un-sun places,
In our sleeping places

Is our sleeplessness, is our restlessness
The result of too much libraries in our heads?
Too much light in the nights of our brains?

We shackle our eyes to the neons of smart phones
To the Google of the new Moses and more
Bringing Ten Commandments and more
From the Tablets of our times
Samsung, Apple, more
Commandments on how to be liked on Facebook
Or followed more on Twitter

At the Gathering of Roads / Mohamed Gibril Sesay

So now we buy needles at night
To thread eyes with overworked fingers
Toiling non-stop in the fields of our keyboards
We have no empathy for our eyes
No empathy for each other's window to the soul
Mornings after the vigils
With our eyes bloody red
With the restlessness of our souls
We ask of our eyes
Why are you so red?

Too much vision too little dreams
For lack of dreams the soul perishes
They who cannot dream well cannot vision well

The mother searches the son's clothes
And picks out those not dirty enough to be laundered
Because she knows
That over-laundering wears out the best
But the stranger searches and orders all be laundered
Ruining the fabrics with much cleansing
Draining the stains of life
From the fabrics of our morals

I am not clean enough I know
Who can never be clean enough
In a world of hot noons and steaming dusts
The placenta that feeds
Is the after-filth
That must be buried

At the Gathering of Roads / Mohamed Gibril Sesay

The other day I saw them
The administrators of God's grant-in-aid
-Or is it grace-in aid? -
To students of the University of Living
Taking bribes before grunting the grant
Many times I doff my heart
To those who go through life
Without divine sponsorship
Their soul may be worn out
Than waist of trousers
Sat on daily and year long
On a sliding fire-stones of Freetown, but hey
They like the sliding

Only some foolish waters think
That its rushing downstream
Would empty the river
Only a fool thinks
He will swim in the same river twice
So is it not the case
That you never meet the same person twice?
Are we all unfaithful
Or are we all polygamists
In that we never make love
To the same person twice

The people of knowledge say
We may be too slow to notice the changes
But everyday is a different me
Every night is a different you

At the Gathering of Roads / Mohamed Gibril Sesay

Let's Eke It Out, Softly

What will the kids
Believe in tomorrow
Will my beliefs today be laughed at
With a cacophony of guffaws?
With taunting references to the values of today?

I move on
Trying to dilute this future laughter
By being a little tolerant here and there
That perchance when the future comes
They may say, well that guy got some sense

But why do I think
I may even be that important
To be a subject even of laughter
What gives me this arrogance
To put myself in the considerations
Of the future
In their laughter or sadness

I trudge on
In a present that is forgetting itself
A generation with receding memories
Begetting a generation with far less memory
Than itself
A generation losing capacities to mourn
A generation losing capacities to make tombstones
A generation without cemeteries

At the Gathering of Roads / Mohamed Gibril Sesay

Without memorials
Without care for what precedes it
Be it good or bad or ugly

Beloved, let's eke it out,
Because we are eking it out
Because it feels fine
Or at least feels less worse
During the eking it out
It may even be fine if
We still have illusions
That we eke it out to be remembered

At the Gathering of Roads / Mohamed Gibril Sesay

A Festival of Press Releases

Elites hauling constitutional stones
At each other's head
Section this section that
Bandaged heads
Turning upon themselves

Amongst the common people
The topic is:
Ar geh de mango
Way me cookery money
Portee new road
Na me turn for geh wata

At the Gathering of Roads / Mohamed Gibril Sesay

Sand and Sound

Let the rays flow
Let the heart tick its own clock
To tell its own time

Mangy bookmen snort our stories
Dirtying our memories
With paws of doom

Residents in the Labyrinth of Alpha Beta
Ill-literate men of letters
Savoring the bent lines from A to Z
Rather than journeying towards
The happy words we could form

A calligraphy of waste
Power-point presentations
Of illuminated stupidities
Wowing worshippers of fonts

Must we heed visionless calligraphers
Making soul-wrenching hermeneutics
Out of the phonemes of our aspirations
Must we obey these ill- literate men of letters
Who transcribe the noisiness of our hopes
Into a calligraphy of phlegm

Must we hearken to the dirge of ringtones
Calling us to answer yes

At the Gathering of Roads / Mohamed Gibril Sesay

To the undertakers of our 'un-destiny'
Lettered men who disemboweled
Pregnancies of hope
To decide academic bets

The Labyrinth of Alpha Beta
Is strewn
With the blood of abortions
The blood of fetal phonemes
That could not become words
That could not become flesh
That could not become our bundle of joy

Manifold rumblings
In the bowels of our hearts
Civil war within
The intestines of meanings
Lettered men constipated with web-links
Forming farts within our souls
Creating piles in the colons of the land
Exposing overturned anuses
As they climb political minarets
To rally their faithful
Their nether-mouths sending foul sounds
Into the ears of our hopes

See the dance of grimace on the face
Of the faithful
As the lettered men
Pierce the bellies of the present
Drawing blood from the un-conceived

At the Gathering of Roads / Mohamed Gibril Sesay

The unborn
And the un-dead

Shut eyes
Sending tears backwards
To the insides of bodies
Through the nostrils
This Liquid sorrowing
Is blocking the path of God's breath
Into the lungs of renewal
God's grace denied access
By verbosities of pessimism
On the cancerous tongues
Of the over-educated under-wise

Waves of putrefaction
Spewing from the chimneys
Of the labyrinthine factories of death
Heat of high degrees
PhDs, MPhils etcetera
Raising the national Fahrenheit
Carbons of rabid tribalists
And font fetishists
Depleting our national ozone

Sea level rising
Sin level rising
Scenes negative expanding
Flooding vast areas
Creating too many islands of vexatious mulling

At the Gathering of Roads / Mohamed Gibril Sesay

Educated buffoons
The doctor deaths of semantics
Fouled mouth Iagos
Mean lettered Lady Macbeths
Mimicking their own grunts
Feeling the sounds
For sighs of affinity
With their foreboding

No way no way
We shall no longer
Be wowed by fonts
No longer genuflect
Before the fetish of letters
We are invading the labyrinth
We ourselves are stringing our phonemes
Into beads of fine hermeneutics
Into songs of freedom

This is our day
We are un-hearing the pessimists
We are giving meanings to our own sounds
Building our own narratives

I stand along this
Beach, this urban sand-scape, this Lumley

A sliver of pleasure
From the sounds
Of my hopes

At the Gathering of Roads

I gather myself within
Like footballers their crotches
On the wall defending a free kick
Few meters from the penalty spot

As our Ramadan advances
The Preacher admonishes
We are also beings of fitra[xv]
Essences of the pure breath
Vultures are nauseated by cleanliness;
The breathing of God within hallows us.
Iblis[xvi] is envious, would not bow,
God's breath nauseates him

At the Gathering of Roads / Mohamed Gibril Sesay

Rainbow-ing of the Clouds (Elections 2012)

What is this?
This evaporation of common sense
Forming web gods
Deluging our commons
With inboxes of doom

And then
Rainbow-ing our clouds
With ICC redress
A Lazarus-ing
By the labyrinthine Christ
Of the Court of Saint Hague of the Netherlands
Can the dead be resurrected by a court?

We in the trenches of the land
Know better
Our land will not be re-doomed
There will be no Lazarus-stench
There shall be no ethnic war
We shall pay no heed
To the masturbatory simulations of war
Hate and doom by cyber-elites
We will not be pushed to war by hate-fonts
On screen-fronts

Our roots are too intertwined
In each other's soil

At the Gathering of Roads / Mohamed Gibril Sesay

We are here ourselves with our children
Not only our foreskins
But the foreskins of our children are buried here
Not only our first teeth
But also those of our children are interred here
Not only us but also our children have made
The sacrifice of the toes' blood
To the stones of the land
To the boromesarr[xvii] of the ancestors
Not only our mothers and sisters
But also our daughters' ears have paid
The blood price to the soil
No ear is more to the ground than theirs
They have paid the ear-price
They dangle the earrings of this matrimony
To the root-efforts of the land
And they tell us
The roots of the land root for peace

Look, the drones of the web-gods
Drop letter bombs for us to open
To our hearts
In front of our children
Here on the ground
In the trenches of the land
While they sit in control rooms
Computer rooms in far-off places
Hehehe-ing the hacked photos
Sent back to mission control
Imagined photos of war during the elections
Of bullets near ballots

At the Gathering of Roads / Mohamed Gibril Sesay

Of blood splattered voter registers
Of everything collapsing
Of J-6 everywhere
Of green bile against red guts
Of gastric wars and ulcerous twists
In the innards of the nation's soul

But we in the trenches know better
There shall be no
Re-doom-ing of this land that we love

At the Gathering of Roads / Mohamed Gibril Sesay

Crutches of Hope

All over the walls of this wounded room
All over the strands of this prayer mat
Are blurred marks
Of what was between us

Blood marks of amputated memories

I feel the pain
At the void
Where the amputated toe of the memory was

I know there was a person like you
A being of love
I know there was a you
But I cannot now
Remember your face

Before college, before philosophy, before the war
Your face was there

But now I hear the sociologists of our story say
That my experience of you
Was suffering from too many superstitions
I hear the surgeons say
That in seeking your face, O God
I cracked my skull
Butting my forehead in the prostrations of prayers
Making my brain vulnerable to all sorts of nonsense

At the Gathering of Roads /Mohamed Gibril Sesay

I hear the doctors say
That I ate too much sugar of your word
Without the insulin of the practical
On the toe of the dreams

The toe that stamps memory
On the grounding of remembering
The toe that brands the skin of our earth
With our sole-marks
The toe that 'umblicals' the placenta
To the nourishments of the new science

So without insulin on the high sugars
Of our toes
A little wound on the toe festered
A little wound from the pellets of agnostic thoughts
And the diabetic toehold
Was amputated
To save my life

But what is life
Without you, O God
Without a memory of how I experienced you
When I was a little boy
Learning the Quran seated near Papa's toe
About the majesty of your loving grace

I move on
Holding crutches of hope
Returning again and again
To this wounded room

At the Gathering of Roads / Mohamed Gibril Sesay

To this matted prayer mat
Forehead on the base of your metaphoric shin
In search of you

But am I not just wasting my longings?
Should I not just resist this urge to return
This search for the guiding contours of your face?
Should I not just accept this receding of guiding memory?
Should I not just embrace this blank visage
That has nothing indicating frown or smile?

Should I not just embrace this desert
And build a new hope
That the other side of that high dune
Is a better place?

The void aches
My hand on the crutches shakes
Hope howls in the wilderness

May the end be beautiful

At the Gathering of Roads /Mohamed Gibril Sesay

I Believe

I believe
Therefore I am

I doubt
Therefore I am not

Money changers at the altars
Of our faith
The imam pronounces their swine halal
For the sacrifice of id ul adha

I doubt
Therefore I am

Preachers pimping faith
Collecting G strings as tithes
Accepting Jifa[xviii] as Zakat

I doubt
Therefore I am my own Imam
In a congregation of one

At the Gathering of Roads /Mohamed Gibril Sesay

He Would Not Be Blackmailed

He heard the call to God
To prayers
But sat it out,
Kissing her

Not that he did not want to go
But he loathed
The meanness in the voice saying
'Prayers are better than women'
The arrogance in the voice
The blackmail about hell and all
He would not be blackmailed unto God

At the Gathering of Roads / Mohamed Gibril Sesay

Let Me Be

Live your holiness
Let me live my less than holy
What has your virginity
Got to do with her whoring?
Must the daughter of a virtuous woman
Be condemned to a life of corseted holiness?
That the pastor's son is an unbeliever, so what?
Was the pastor's grandfather Christ?
Should I eat off the Imam's feet
Because my soul is ill?

Don't preach to me about
I living a life with God spelled backwards
Would you use that
To justify using your holy rod
To strike apart our pubes
Like some urchin do to copulating dogs
At the junctions of our lives?
Must you be some Moses
Cutting my sea
To let your holy followers
Stampede through my wound?

Go preach to yourself and let me be
Does your quoting holy give you the right
To blare your loudspeaker into our night?
Why must you rave about my grave
Are you the landlord of my tomb?

At the Gathering of Roads / Mohamed Gibril Sesay

Are you the owner of her womb?
Are you our grave-lord?
Do you hold the title deed to my umbilical cord?

Let me be, let me be
You have your religion
I have my decision

At the Gathering of Roads / Mohamed Gibril Sesay

I Have Seen It Before

I have seen it before
Long ago in the future
The beast slouches towards its genitals
To generate its kind

But our people say
The womb brings out
The pastor and the thief
The world, some say
Is saved by slaughter
- of a manly god who is also a godly man

Avoid the extremes, beloved
That when evil comes it comes weak
That when good comes, it comes not with the fury
Of a hurricane on our hill-perched souls

At the Gathering of Roads / Mohamed Gibril Sesay

As our Ramadan advances,
I gather myself within,
Like Bilkis[xix] her skirt
On stepping on Solomon's glassy floor.

As Our Ramadan advances
The imagination becomes hungrier,
Many travellers have fallen off the Sirati[xx] of faith
Into he imagination's insatiability

But the holy books say we are born to choose
That's the divine right of humans
And born to choose means born to imagine possibilities
Do the woolen ones, the Sufi
Not say there are as many paths to God
As are human souls

Save that this faith, this new strain, clogs all other paths,
Save one – the straight path,
Submission to the weal of the caliph.

Woe then unto poets
Howls the fanatic
Don't you see how their sayings suggest too many possibilities?
Don't you see them twist their mouths
To change the sounds of words?
How they wring their lines to confuse straight readers?

At the Gathering of Roads / Mohamed Gibril Sesay

On Being Commissioned to Pray
(February 1993)

now
there is a national prayer committee
commissioned to promote
prayers and fasting
and other mysticisms they say
make god have mercy

as if our misery
is from the good lord

i'm sick
with this plowing of the air
long time we've been planting
our seeds in heaven
still no harvest
what harvest?
manna? quail?
they're not our staple food
rice is

to hell to heaven

i'm sick and tired
with this game of apology to god
for what we do to ourselves

what a great misplacement of hands

At the Gathering of Roads / Mohamed Gibril Sesay

Aberdeen Beach

I am here again
The sea shoring my imagination
Listening to songs
'Bout the eternal dance
Of man and woman
On the waves of destiny

Some go under the swell
Drowned by the sweet foolishness
Of clasping the leaves of love
For salvation

What will I be saved by in this raging existence?

I grasp the rotting log
Of the admonished certainty
The log is tossed about, but still afloat
I hold on to the log of ark
But my dreams are drowning
Happiness sacrificed by daggers of advice
Wrought by the ritualists of normalcy

But shall I continue
Jonah-ing my dreams
That we may safely arrive
On the shores of my safest death
And thence to the necropolis of the advised tomb
And the epitaph:

At the Gathering of Roads / Mohamed Gibril Sesay

'This Mufti-man took the straight path to death
He never drank the alcohol of dreams
He lived a long life of received wisdom
And established virtues'

But of what use are epitaphs to corpses
At what cost these promises of safe death
Of what relevance is life lived long
In the torture chambers of antediluvian advice
Yoked with Noah's beasts
In the ark of the stern

I unshackle the manacles of the coin-mint
Stamp on the adored faces of the money-print
Grab an Africa size pint
Get damn drunk on dreams
Jump off the narratives of ark
And let go the rotting logs of
Marriage
Profession
Religion
And many more

At the Gathering of Roads / Mohamed Gibril Sesay

Waters Loll

Waters loll in the dunes
Of desert-times

Listen
Imagination makes water-myths flow
Not viscosity

Gideon knows that their waterways
Are also their faith-ways
That they who dip face in water
Have but faith that is smaller than couscous-seed
They cannot be warriors of the lord
Pharoah dips face in a water-clearing
Moses does the same
But faith makes Moses and hosts survive
Pharoah drowns

Preacher-man also says
Sinners shall drown in hell-wells
Deeper than a whole-day–imagining-of–depth

Former-times the Bayti[xxi] runs
The gauntlet to the river of ablutions[xxii]
Mornings, the water is like fire
On unhealed penises
Water scorch-heals penises
-baptism to African faith ways

At the Gathering of Roads / Mohamed Gibril Sesay

In Grandparent's times they say
Rain falls even on oceans
Urging reluctant prior-eaters to join meals again

Not now- waters are rough
So we–in boat-in-the-middle-of-stormy-waters say
To famishing no-swimmers on shore, 'come let's eat'

That's the new generosity of water-call

At the Gathering of Roads / Mohamed Gibril Sesay

We March-on

Pieces of memory
For borderposts

On a page
A word is bordered by emptiness

Inspeechit'sthememory of speaker/hearer

Thearabs say
Acquire another language
You acquire another memory

How true how true
We marchon with our un-native accents
Un-native orthographies
Changing wordscapes
Colonising memories
Soyinka is our cortez

In france theAcademy
Reviews residentialpermits
Of alienwords
The Africa poet[xxiii] who helps them
Is our Trojan horse

We marchon
Jonathan swift foresaw this
And cried for an English Academy

At the Gathering of Roads / Mohamed Gibril Sesay

This Computer is that dream come true
I wish it babel`s fate for daring to say Sesay
Is really SASSY or SAUCY or…
Back to the programmers
You never learnt my mama tongue

At the Gathering of Roads / Mohamed Gibril Sesay

Wines of Memories

Must we make bad strong wine
From our rotting memories
Of war, slavery and all that
And get so drunk on them
We cannot stay steady
Cannot stay focus
On the tasks of the day

Alcohol content too high
Disabling our sanity
Drunken Fathers exposing loins
To drunken daughters
Incestuous fun
In the African sun
Giving birth to genetic freaks

Must the alcohol content of memories
Be so strong
Can't we have better distillers
Of wines for finer joy
Listening to the kondi and balanji[xxiv]
Honoring the newest born
Of the race
With better griots
Inspiring us with better ways
Of telling
In better verses
With better tunes?

At the Gathering of Roads / Mohamed Gibril Sesay

As our Ramadan advances,

I pray, O faith, I yearn your certitude, hopeful.

Hoping is dreaming with eyes wide open
To the ultra-violet of Sun-god Ra.
Miranda[xxv] on the Island of the living witch.
That the Father and his Ariels[xxvi] are around
Is an epic lie told by an English poet
To calm the wretchedness of being flung upon yourself

Look out, o beloved,
The moralist is the being of the after-here
Stranded on the shores of now.
Maturity, they say,
Is the downsizing of hope, retrenching dreams.
What do you eat, grace or grass?

Stomach like man who has been gbagba[xxvii]-ed
Rectum knotted by evil ones
We have been told for too long
That grass and grace are not on speaking terms
That grace is up and grass is down.
Is that really so?
Are purity and impurity mutually exclusive?
Just reflect your being
Is it not made of gore and glow?
Shit and spirit?
Soil and soul?

At the Gathering of Roads / Mohamed Gibril Sesay

But what do you glory in
Grass or grace, which do you assert?

At the Gathering of Roads /Mohamed Gibril Sesay

The Raw Millennium

Memories of
1900 to 1999
The century of cemeteries
Weal our will

And the new millennium is already gashed
Festering in the oily spaces
Of Sudan and Iraq

Sores opening
In private places
Now wired unto public spaces

The Bush-man of Texas
Crowns himself
Gynecologist
And intrude
Into our pubic conversations

And draw out
From deep within wombs
Fetuses deformed by mental scalpels
To justify
Abortions of futures

At the Gathering of Roads / Mohamed Gibril Sesay

Stick the stems
In the soil of cells
Let's re-search
For the healing manioc
Below the stem (sowed in our) cells

At the Gathering of Roads / Mohamed Gibril Sesay

Freedom of Thought

Have you ever
Thought of doing:

In a class
You remove your trouser

In some mosque
You loudly cuss the imam

In some church
You in full view pee on the sacraments

Or on the road you throw your head
At some 100 miles per hour wheels of some truck

Have your ever had
That inner joy of free thought

That scaling of the hurdles
Of thoughts

You may not act it out
But ah
The inner playfulness
Of dribbling thoughts
In the mind-fields?

At the Gathering of Roads / Mohamed Gibril Sesay

Rain Dark[xxviii]

When rain dark
wishes drizzle
on mortal man condition

'Rain don't come
my headside[xxix] leaks
my waistside[xxx] too'

'Rain come
for our taps have gone on leave
prior to retirement'

'Rain don't come
it's hard to dreg[xxxi]
in the smell smell mud'

'Rain come
that the by-day woman[xxxii]
may not come'

Rain dark
What do you drizzle?

At the Gathering of Roads / Mohamed Gibril Sesay

As our Ramadan advances,

Hunger eats the insides of our vision
The way our people say witches eat the insides of a child
The child is now hollow than an upside down calabash,
Frailer than dangling phlegm

So as our Ramadan advances,
The Preachers conspire to keep our vision steady.
They say: keep vigil, tend your end
Pray the nightly Tahajud[xxxiii]
S/he who is awake cannot be bewitched.

At the Gathering of Roads / Mohamed Gibril Sesay

Madam she

(by Kill Them The Great)

I look and look and look
Me eye full up
But I still look
I look and look and look
Me eye begin for vomit looking
I begin for rub nasty looking all side of her
So Madam she speak
I tell you
John Bull tell lie
"Why are you looking at me like that?"
"Eeee eye get boundary? How you manage know I look you?
"I saw you looking at me."
"Meself see you"
Madam She speak more and more and more
She say I get untidy eye and latrine mouth
Me heart warm
I will not let her fit her eye on me
So I speak to tell her I can speak
I say
"Madam She
Why are you making pomposity
As if you cannot contaminate with the man?"
aaah… that go inside her bone
whirl like talabi
and I begin for hear big big English

At the Gathering of Roads / Mohamed Gibril Sesay

I hear and hear and hear
Me ear belly burst
But madam she still speak
Still whirl like talabi
… bra I tell you
madam she fine O
fine like a thing for eat
but when madam she whirl
agbado agbado [xxxiv]tell lie
… bra forget bout her
Even if she want you
she go only wrap and wrap you head
like you get scrap head
and give you sweat
to her bookman
Them all hate we
Them and them men
Only rain bring we and them
Under one roof

At the Gathering of Roads / Mohamed Gibril Sesay

September 16, 2015

Our land drank too much
Of the alcohol of rain

She had been wobbling
Towards this big rum-bar
Gutting her liver
In the little taverns along the way

So when the big bar of rain
Opens its doors
Unto her gaping mouth
Her liver was too weak
To drain out the alcohol of ruin
Her pregnancies of citizens
Washed down her thighs

It was blood over
Blood from the gutted insides of my Freetown
Alluvium of flesh and ruin
All over the body of the land

At the Gathering of Roads /Mohamed Gibril Sesay

We Tie Them Neat Neat

See them writer squeal
Like chalk on hard bad board
See them day so rife
Beating down this doggy doggy life
With them sledge hammer
The holler-call the imagination

Dog dream stays in dog belly
So good for this doggy doggy world
But them writer nor understand this
See them raise leg to piss
Them dream of a dog-free world
On we doggy doggy civilization

So we tie neat neat them crazy dog
Inside rice-bag and fling to bog

At the Gathering of Roads / Mohamed Gibril Sesay

At the Gathering of Roads

I gather myself within
Like tired worshippers their hands
Whilst standing up for the long verses
Of our Tahajud
Wobbling knees
Tired ankles
Shackled to the holiness
Of the Imam's voice

Ambrose, remember
There were a number of us,
At the Bistrot de Paris[xxxv]
When I asked Peter
About the last ten days of his Ramadan.
He said, I'll keep vigil in the cathedrals of England,
Restore the ancient chandeliers,
Put olive oil to fire the wick-glow
Now threatened by the waves of this electricity age.

Sometimes I think the vigils of the West are easier,
It's like a conscience imposed anger at their own kind
of mess.
Have you ever had a conscience imposed hunger?
They only offer pigs genitals. You wouldn't ch-
Eat, wouldn't baikorkor.
So your belly eats the muscles of your thighs,
Churns your voice wavering like a broadcaster's in an
ill-tuned radio.

At the Gathering of Roads / Mohamed Gibril Sesay

You shut your eyes;
You see a delicious plate of angels.
You grab it
You open your eyes.
O, the plate is gone.
Hunger now assails you like frenzy drummers a drum;
The sounds of your hollowness reverberates the world.
O beloved, if the drum is not hollow,
How would the drummers fare?
What would our world dance to?
The piano?
O my Ambiguous Adventures.
Hunger, says Hamidou Kane in his Ambiguous Adventures
Is the principal enemy of God (p11, p82).
Pawpaw, our people say, is no Kombra[xxxvi]
To the inhabitants of the hungry season.

At the Gathering of Roads / Mohamed Gibril Sesay

Customs of Fell Deeds

And dreadful objects so familiar
That mothers shall but smile when they behold
Their infants quartered with the hands of war
All pity choked by a custom of fell deeds`
            Shakespeare

Yesterday
I laughed
When I heard
They chopped off his ears
And gave them to him
As New Year present

…flayed soles
cleaved skulls
cut hands
breasts
limbs
Seven women
All naked
Burst upon us
With tales of savage rapes
And slit napes

And the severed head
Dancing bouncing

At the Gathering of Roads / Mohamed Gibril Sesay

Towards the net
…evil has scored another goal

And we spectators
And spectacle
Shout for revenge
Urging our players
To score similar goals.

At the Gathering of Roads / Mohamed Gibril Sesay

Roaches Guns and Peace

I'm a civilian, though
not as military men say,
a bloody civilian. I'm a bloodless
civilian, a cockroach; I
love books, I
sulk in night
corners afraid of the light
that illuminates the books. I
read in the doom,
of the gloom
of the closet teaming with my mind,
crowded with my kind
I'm a roach, I
know my place. Lacking blood I
don't interfere in a butchers'
palaver. I

hate guns,
 goons with guns
gunning gutter guys dock –
ing
further
down
into the piss
to save head –
more peace-
ful than split skulls drying teeth
under the sun.

At the Gathering of Roads / Mohamed Gibril Sesay

Survival Dream

The woman crouches
In the undergrowth
Peeping at cracked souls
On the prowl

Her dream
Is security for her child
And a school
And a playground
A friend
A brother

Just some ordinary things
Pots
Plates
A place to tell her dreams
Her hopes

Hands to plait her hair
Feet to dance
And go to the market
Or to the stream
Or tap yonder

Perhaps a husband
That listens to the language
Of her heart

At the Gathering of Roads / Mohamed Gibril Sesay

A man whose worth's not measured
By the blows on her back

Just these ordinary …
Receding now
In the dream
Of the woman
In the undergrowth

At the Gathering of Roads / Mohamed Gibril Sesay

I shook my head; moaned

(on reading Rami Ditzani`s
A BRAND SNATCHED FROM ANTI –TANK
FIRE

At Naconquer`s outdooring
In the noonsun
The starving treeshade lolling at me streaming inside a
jean jacket in the crypt of this poem - sepulchral
words of a boy dying, a father fighting tears giving him
the last drops as he wipes the drops of
         W   t
         A   e
         T   a
         E   r
         R   s
Off the chest of the little boy burnt to the very soul by
the dragon-belch of avaricious war-gods
Father weeps
As he prays
Boy dies
As father throbs for deliverance)

As famishing shadows
Writhe in a fratricidal noon

At the Gathering of Roads /Mohamed Gibril Sesay

Orders from Below
(February 1996)

They kick your mother
ORDERS FROM ABOVE
They detain journalists
ORDERS FROM ABOVE
They sack her husband
ORDERS FROM ABOVE
They grow F-A-T
ORDERS FROM ABOVE
And fart on us
ORDERS FROM ABOVE
We grow thin
ORDER FROM ABOVE
And become things
ORDERS FROM ABOVE
They seize the wares of traders
ORDERS FROM ABOVE
And give them to their girl friends
ORDERS FROM ABOVE
They underpay teachers
ORDERS FROM ABOVE
Nurses and Civil Servants
ORDERS FROM ABOVE
They over reward…..

P ACK UP AND GO
ORDERS FROM BELOW

At the Gathering of Roads / Mohamed Gibril Sesay

At the Gathering of Roads

I gather myself within
Like feet of experienced mosque sitters
Soles touching under-thighs
Heels almost butting the under-loins

At the gathering of roads
At the gathering of destinies
At the gathering of possibilities
At the gathering of imaginations
I gather myself within
Like the cupped palms of the faithful
Saying Ameen[xxxvii]
To the Dua[xxxviii] of the Imam

And I ask
But what if the hunger is voluntary,
Like in this Ramadan
Would you break your prostrations for koko-ebeh[xxxix]
Would you fast forward the alfatiha
To eat sara of ritual murderers?

O God my God
Grant me will to pray my Tahajud
And may our end be beautiful!

At the Gathering of Roads / Mohamed Gibril Sesay

[i] Muslim Friday Congregational prayers
[ii] Krio for 'child'
[iii] Subhi and Magrib; dawn and evening prayers in Islam
[iv] Parts into which Islamic obligatory prayers are divided
[v] Funeral prayers
[vi] Prostration
[vii] Opening chapter of the Koran, read in almost every Muslim supplications
[viii] Offering, charity
[ix] Hiding to eat whilst fasting, but maintaining in public that you are fasting
[x] Themne belief relating to dead witches and wizards coming back to torment the living
[xi] Whip made of hides
[xii] High Officials of Poro, the secret society charged with putting an end to the menace of resurrecting witches and wizards
[xiii] Woman just out of the initiation ceremony, a paragon of beauty
[xiv] Reference to how the exhumed corpse is cut into pieces to put an end to the menace
[xv] In Islam 'state of purity, everybody being born pure, without sin'
[xvi] In the Koran, another name for Satan
[xvii] sacred stones at the center of the Themne conceptions of the divine
[xviii] Unclean meat
[xix] In Koranic exegesis, name for the Queen of Sheba
[xx] In Islamic eschatology, bridge over hell that all must pass through on Day of Judgment. Those with faith cross very fast, those with little faith take a while, and those without fall off in to hell
[xxi] Themne for 'male circumcision initiate'
[xxii] In some Themne male circumcision ritual, the initiate runs through a gauntlet of whip holding men to the river where their sores are washed
[xxiii] Senghor was a member of the French Academy that certified acceptable French words every year

At the Gathering of Roads / Mohamed Gibril Sesay

[xxiv] Musical instruments
[xxv] In Shakespeare's 'The Tempest,' a young woman almost all alone on an Island
[xxvi] Reference to Ariel, a goodly spirit in Shakespeare's **'The Tempest'**
[xxvii] Belief about constipation induced by evil ones, often resulting in death from a swollen belly
[xxviii] Krio for 'when clouds darken'
[xxix] Krio expression for 'the head of the bed'
[xxx] Krio for 'foot of the bed'
[xxxi] Krio for 'eke out a living'
[xxxii] Woman creditor who asks for repayment on a daily basis
[xxxiii] Very long night prayers during the last ten days of Ramadan
[xxxiv] Very active masked spirit
[xxxv] Restaurant in downtown Freetown, now closed
[xxxvi] Suckling woman, benevolent woman, a mother
[xxxvii] Amen
[xxxviii] Islamic supplication
[xxxix] Trifle

www.ingramcontent.com/pod-product-compliance
Lightning Source LLC
Chambersburg PA
CBHW032206040426
42449CB00005B/467